CW00433519

A Mother's Prayer Journal

Being Loved and Loving Well

By Perry-May Britton

© Perry-May

INTRODUCTION

It always astonishes me that the most famous woman of all time and around the world is probably Mary, the mother of Jesus. She was an unassuming, humble Jewish girl and yet became WORLD famous throughout history, simply for being a mother. A mother! She carried Jesus in her womb, gave birth to him and then watched over him as he grew up. She treasured all that he did in her heart. She was a fearless young woman who said 'yes' to God. She was full of faith and she was highly favoured. I want to be like her.

Before I became a parent myself (when I was 42!), I fostered a young girl. She fell into my life unexpectedly, before I was married, and I didn't really know what I was doing. I was surrounded by wonderful friends who prayed for me and supported me. One of them sent me this verse from Isaiah 40:11: 'he gently leads those that have young'. It is one of the verses which I have grown to lean on over and over again, both as a foster parent, and now as I have my own child. It is the hardest and the best job in the whole world, and I need all the help I can get.

Whether you carried your child in your own womb or grew one in your heart (through fostering, adoption or as a stepmother), this little journal is designed to help you find space in your day to pray for yourself, your circumstances and your family; to help you love them better, seek God for them and ensure the environment in which they grow is a 'thin' place where God is welcomed. Hopefully it will help you to tackle some of the spiritual aspects of being a mother, and will also give you some practical ideas or actions you can do as prophetic acts to partner with the Lord for breakthrough.

My prayer is that you will grow in love and connection with God and with your family, whatever shape they are.

God bless you in your journey.

Perry-May

ABOUT THE AUTHOR

This little journal was written and illustrated by Perry-May Britton. She is married to Mike, and she is a mum to Joshua and they live in a little cottage in rural England. They love people, entertaining and living simply. They have one small dog and a large flock of cheeky chickens.

Perry-May knows and loves Jesus and takes great delight in helping others grow deeper in their relationship with him.

You can find out more on www.perry-may.com

HOW TO USE THIS JOURNAL

Each day there is a short **bible reading**, some ideas for your **journal**, an **action** and / or an encouragement to **pray**. You will need at least five minutes, a modern translation of the bible and something to write with. You could do this alone or with a group of other mothers.

The readings are intended to highlight one or two small points but if you have time, it is always good to read around the verse, discover the context in which it was written, and invest in your knowledge of the bible.

There are four sections:
- Preparing your heart
- Preparing your home
- Loving your family well
- Trials and tribulations

You do not have to do it in order but pick the theme most relevant for you at the time.

EACH DAY:

READ THE PASSAGE

You could read it out aloud several times slowly or you could try reading it in different versions of the bible. If you have time, read the whole chapter or find out the context in which it is written. Good questions to ask yourself as you read are: What does this say? What does it mean? And how does it apply to me?

JOURNAL IDEA

It is entirely up to you what you write. You can follow the suggestions or simply write down what you feel the Lord is speaking to you about. I sometimes like to write down the verses that jump out at me or just doodle and enjoy the time being with the Lord!

PRAYER / ACTION

I love doing small prophetic acts because they help me ground my faith journey. They show God that I really mean business and create helpful memories that link to truth. A prophetic act is like a baptism or a handshake – it is a symbolic act with meaning. Prayer is very personal and it doesn't matter how you pray, all that matters is that you do!

You are a WONDERMAMMA!

SECTION ONE

Preparing your heart

This section is all about you! Who you are in God's eyes and how he promises to lead and guide you as you parent your child. In the business of everyday life, it is really easy to forget that YOU are important and that your relationship with the Lord will affect everything. Use these readings to remember that you are highly favoured in God's eyes and that despite its difficulties, being a mum is a huge privilege.

DAY ONE: You are God's child

READ: Hebrews 2:6-7

JOURNAL IDEA: Before you were given the name 'mother' you were a child of God. That child is still in there! Before we allow any other labels: mother, wife, overweight, employee, black, white, divorced or anything, the best thing we can do for ourselves and for our family is be who we were made to be. Before thinking about being a mum – remind yourself who you are in Christ.

Put on your crown
Your Dad is THE
KING !

PRAYER / ACTION: Crowns are great symbols! Make or buy yourself a crown - it can be a paper crown or a priceless tiara. Pop it on your head and wear it around the house remembering who you are: a child of the King of Kings!

DAY TWO: You are highly favoured

READ: Luke 1:30-35

JOURNAL IDEA: Imagine what it must have been like to be Mary: highly favoured, assigned with carrying and parenting the son of God. Write about the day you knew you were going to become a mother - how you felt, who you told etc.

PRAYER / ACTION: Whatever the circumstances surrounding the arrival of your child, having them in your life is a sign of God's favour on you. Take some time to thank him for his favour and decide to step into his favour again. You could even literally take a large step forward as a prophetic act to show God you are wanting to step into/remain in his favour.

DAY THREE: Treasure in your heart

READ: Luke 2:19

JOURNAL IDEA: Isn't this the heart of a mother — treasuring memories in her heart? Write about some of your most special memories of your child. When we fill our hearts with true treasures we become so much richer ourselves.

Treasure in your
heart ♡.

PRAYER / ACTION: Start a notebook for each of your children and use it to add funny anecdotes, stories or milestones and the moments you treasure about them. Write down anything that your child does that makes you laugh. Your children will LOVE it when you read it back to them. It will make them feel loved and special and will be something which they will treasure when they are older.

DAY FOUR: Worship with thanks

READ: Luke 1:46-55

JOURNAL IDEA: Write about all the things you are thankful for in your child or write a poem / song of worship giving thanks to God for your child. Thankfulness is such a powerful tool - it opens doors and breaks down barriers, it can change atmospheres and soften hearts.

Worship with your whole being.

PRAYER / ACTION: Find a time to tell your child how thankful you are to have them in your life, eg. 'I am so grateful that you are in my life, you give me so much joy and laughter. God was really kind when he gave you to me!' It is amazing how much children need to hear this.

DAY FIVE: God will guide you

READ: Isaiah 40:9-11

JOURNAL IDEA: Take some time to write out the areas in your parenting where you really need the Lord to 'gently lead' you.

PRAYER / ACTION: Light a candle and watch it for a while. God is a light for your path. Give the Lord your journal page - ask him to be in each area you have highlighted.

DAY SIX: Children are a heritage

READ: PSALM 127:3

JOURNAL IDEA: Heritage can mean 'a special possession'. Write about the special possessions you have that you want to pass on to your child. It can be physical things, but also gifts, skills or passions.

PRAYER / ACTION: Carve out a little space in your day today to spend on your knees before the Lord. Ask him to show you how to pass on to your child the wonderful heritage which you carry.

DAY SEVEN: Lean on God

READ: Proverbs 3:5-6

JOURNAL IDEA: Sometimes I find parenting makes no sense! When I think I have got it just right, everything seems to go wrong, and sometimes when I am sure that I made mistakes, somehow the outcome can be really good! How much do you lean on your own understanding? Take some time to write what it means to trust the Lord with all your heart in all aspects concerning your child.

"I'm sticking close to the good shepherd."

PRAYER / ACTION: Next time you feel anxious about an aspect of parenting, stop, breathe and take a moment to choose to trust God. With him you can make good decisions and you can trust him with your child. Somehow he can make your paths straight even in the most difficult parenting terrain. Go for a walk with the Lord, make it an act of choosing to give God permission to direct your steps.

DAY EIGHT: Fearless mother

READ: Proverbs 31:25

JOURNAL IDEA: How wonderful to be able to laugh at the days to come! It is very easy to let fear creep into our parenting: fear of failure, fear of the future and many other fears. The Lord wants us to laugh with joy about our future. Take some time to confess your fears to the Lord and choose to laugh at them and beyond them into your future!

PRAYER / ACTION: Laughter is infectious and powerful! It can change your mood and the atmosphere. Next time you are alone, start laughing out loud - fake it until you find yourself actually giggling! Then imagine you are laughing at the days to come. It may sound a bit mad, but it is a spiritual activity that can bring transformation. Then, if you are feeling brave, do it at dinner with your family and see what happens! Teach your children to laugh over their fears.

Draw yourself laughing...

DAY NINE: They call her blessed

READ: Proverbs 31:27-28

JOURNAL IDEA: How precious to have a child that wakes in the mornings and calls you blessed! This perfect morning is far from our experience and this perfect Proverbs 31 woman is quite elusive to me. But there is something exciting about reaching out towards her. Write a prayer asking God to help you lean into the qualities of this woman.

Note: There is NO CONDEMNATION in there. If reading this makes you feel terrible about yourself, then ask God to give you his eyes, and look at yourself as he sees you. He loves you completely.

"Blessed Mamma!"

PRAYER / ACTION: Read the rest of the description of the Proverbs 31 woman. Choose something that she does and begin to put it into practice.

DAY TEN: Take me to higher ground

READ: Psalm 61:2-3

JOURNAL IDEA: In order to parent well, we really need God's help to stand on higher ground, to see what he sees and to have the peace that he has. Think of something that is feeling overwhelming or where you are feeling out of your depth and take a moment to ask God to help you up onto 'the rock'. Look at the situation from that perspective and write what you can see.

Stand on
higher ground...
and look.

PRAYER / ACTION: Literally stand on a rock or at the top of stairs, climb a hill or a mountain - just find a high place and look down. Then ask God to speak to you.

DAY ELEVEN:
Let the children come to Jesus

READ: Matthew 19: 13-15

JOURNAL IDEA: How can we make it easy for our children to have access to Jesus? He longs to bless them. Write about what you already see of the kingdom of heaven in your child.

PRAYER / ACTION: Call the glimpses of God's kingdom into being over your child, eg. you could say things like: 'I can see that you are kind / hope-filled / gentle / a leader / an encourager / a logical thinker (whatever quality or gift you see). What a gift you have!'

Use your hands to bless them and give the appropriate assurance with physical touch, just like Jesus did: take their hand, kiss them, stroke their shoulders / back, give them a big bear hug. Sometimes all they need is a little reassurance without words.

DAY TWELVE:
Comparison - the thief of joy

READ: 1 Samuel 16:7

JOURNAL IDEA: Comparing ourselves, our child and our parenting with others is very destructive, makes us feel bad about ourselves or our situation, and damages friendships. The main problem with comparison is that we compare our insides to other people's outsides. We look at the outward appearance BUT GOD LOOKS AT THE HEART!

Lay down your comparison now, today. Lay it down. Put your heart into being the best mum you can be for YOUR child and God will be so pleased.

Man looks at the outside

PRAYER / ACTION: If comparison has been a difficult issue for you, it may help to pray it through with someone you trust. This is one to leave at the cross. No one benefits from carrying it around.

A little doodle page!

SECTION TWO

Preparing your home

This section is all about setting up your home for success!

Every few years take some time to 'reclaim' your home for the Lord. We want it to be a vibrant place full of life, hospitality, creativity, fun and joy. We want the Holy Spirit to be welcome and for God's word to be spoken freely.

By paying attention to our home regularly, we are creating a place where our child feels safe, loved and known. We want it to be a place of hospitality and ensure that whoever crosses our threshold knows they are safe and welcomed.

No matter what your home life is like, many of these prayers as well as simple, practical things, can make a huge difference and change the atmosphere. For example, if your child suffers nightmares, you can see great results by reclaiming your home and changing the atmosphere. This is a real gift we can give to our children. It is a way we can quietly invest in our family life.

DAY THIRTEEN: Set your door frame

READ: Joshua 24:15 and Deuteronomy 6:4-9

JOURNAL IDEA: You could write out Joshua 24:15b or a favourite verse as a declaration over your family and then turn it into a written prayer, eg. 'Lord, it is my heart's desire that everyone who lives in my household knows you and serves you. Thank you, Lord, for hearing my prayer'.

My home - a place of blessing!

PRAYER / ACTION: Write or print out some verses and stick them on your door frame. Take a moment to stand at your front door – the threshold of your home - and pray. Pray about what comes in and what goes out of the door and ask him if there are any more specific verses he would like you to pray over this threshold. Invite the Holy Spirit in and declare truth over the entrance of your home.

DAY FOURTEEN: Set the atmosphere

READ: Acts 16:25-34

JOURNAL IDEA: What impact has worship had on you in the past? Have you had an experience of being set free by its power? Or a memorable encounter with the Lord in worship? Write about the experience.

PRAYER / ACTION: Set up some worship music to play in your home for a whole day even while you are not in it. Do this particularly in your child's room. As you let the worship wash through your home, pray that it would break the chains of anything binding, that it would bring peace, comfort and great joy to your family.

DAY FIFTEEN: Put truth on the walls

READ: 1 Chronicles 28:11-18

JOURNAL IDEA: Did you realise that God actually cares about the spaces we inhabit? Write what you think about the details of your own home and how you think God sees it.

PRAYER / ACTION: Draw, write, print or purchase some biblical truth to put on your walls. Children pick up on the smallest of things. Pray your child will learn the truth you have posted around the house and that they will learn to love God's word.

It may also be that God is asking you to think about other aspects of your home eg. wake up 10 minutes early for a week and pray in a different room each day or make a prayer corner/room/chair. Whatever he says, it is always best to just do it!

DAY SIXTEEN: Invite angels

READ: Psalm 91:9-13

JOURNAL IDEA: Write out the areas you would particularly like the Lord to send his angels on behalf of your family.

There are angels all around you.

PRAYER / ACTION: Imagine angels around your child. Invite God's angelic forces to surround your child especially in the times / seasons that you are unable to protect them. This really helps as our children get older, trusting that God will send an army of angels to guard around them.

DAY SEVENTEEN: Address the adult relationships

READ: Romans 12:16 (if you have time read verses 9-21)

JOURNAL IDEA: What would it mean for you to live in harmony with the other adults in your household? Write a blessing for the father/father figure of your child. (If you are unable to do that, then write a prayer for your child to have healthy relationships with male role models).

PRAYER / ACTION: Take time to pray about or resolve to work out how to live well with your partner / other adults in your home. Our children learn more from us by watching us than by our 'teaching' them with words. One of the best gifts you could ever give them is adult relationships that honour one another and show consistent respect and kindness.

Have another little doodle!

SECTION THREE

Loving your family well

It is our dream that we will raise a child who has a personal relationship with the Lord, and that out of that he is confident to live well. We try to offer faith in a way that is accessible and understandable.

This section is about finding ways to love your child into God's kingdom, about helping them to navigate the world they find themselves in and guiding them appropriately.

You may be thinking 'my child is too old for this', but our children are NEVER too old for some encouragement; never too old to know that they are loved; never too old to be prayed over; never too old for us to declare God's truth in their lives; never too old to call out God's gold in each one of them.

DAY EIGHTEEN: Your child is known

READ: Psalm 139: 16

JOURNAL IDEA: Ask God to begin to reveal to you some of the beautiful things he knows about your child. Write them down so you can treasure them in your heart and pray them into being.

PRAYER / ACTION: You could read the whole of this Psalm as a prayer / declaration over your child. What a wonderful thing to know that God knows EVERYTHING about them, and that he is with them.

DAY NINETEEN: Your child's calling

READ: Jeremiah 1:4-5

JOURNAL IDEA: Just like Jeremiah was set apart and appointed as a prophet, so God has a plan for your child. Take some time to ask the Lord to begin to reveal to you some of the things he has planned and appointed for your child. It is so much easier and more fruitful to pray God's will into being for our children than to pray our wishes / desires for them.

PRAYER / ACTION: It is a good idea to pray with someone about this, perhaps your husband or prayer partner. Call out the GOLD in your child in prayer, eg. 'Thank you Lord, that you have made my child to be skilled with their hands / have a vision for the world / to be a natural teacher. I pray, Lord, that you would nurture and nourish him/her and his/her gifts so that he/she is able to flourish. Open doors for him/her that bring great joy and satisfaction'.

DAY TWENTY:
Pass on God's faithfulness

READ: Isaiah 38:19

JOURNAL IDEA: After he recovered from his illness Hezekiah wrote this song. We – the 'LIVING' – must praise God and tell our children about his faithfulness. Write how you could show or tell your child about God's faithfulness.

PRAYER / ACTION: Prepare to tell your testimony to your children and always be ready to give it. Pray for opportunities to speak about your faith with them. Maybe whilst walking to school, in the car or over a meal. It doesn't need to be a big and intense conversation.

DAY TWENTY-ONE:
Flourish and be blessed

READ: Psalm 115:14-15

JOURNAL IDEA: God wants you AND your child to flourish, he wants you to succeed. Write what it would mean for you and your family to flourish.

PRAYER / ACTION: This is a great prayer to speak out loud over your child. Speak God's blessing to them; whisper it to them or declare it over them when they are asleep… 'The Lord wants you to flourish, [*insert their name*]. The Lord, the maker of heaven and earth wants to bless you'.

DAY TWENTY-TWO:
Start them off well

READ: Proverbs 22:6

JOURNAL IDEA: This is a wonderful promise. It means parenting should not be a burden. Our job is to start them off well, set them on course and then trust that God will take on the rest. Write about what this means for you.

PRAYER / ACTION: Simply by having this book you are already taking positive steps for your child. A fun prophetic act you could do is to write your dreams / visions for your child on a piece of paper, turn it into a paper boat, put it on some water (a stream, lake, pond or even the bath!), and push it off. As you do that, pray that you are starting them off well.

DAY TWENTY-THREE:
You can't do it alone

READ: Proverbs 17:6

JOURNAL IDEA: Your child is 'a crown' for their grandparents. What a beautiful picture! Write a prayer that your child would have a great relationship with their grandparents / aunts / uncles / cousins etc.

PRAYER / ACTION: Take some time to invest in your child's relationship with their extended family. If possible, help them to see one another regularly (even if you are just using technology), and ensure there are photos around the house to help your child feel part of a bigger picture. [If you do not have extended family, you could 'adopt' friends / your community / your church to be part of your child's 'family', ensuring they have healthy relationships with others not just their peers].

DAY TWENTY-FOUR:
Moved by the Spirit

READ: Luke 2:27-32

JOURNAL IDEA: Jesus' parents are such a faithful example to us. Perhaps you had your child formally dedicated or baptised? Whether you did or not, write a prayer of dedication giving your child to the Lord.

"God is so pleased with you!"

PRAYER / ACTION: If you feel it is appropriate, speak to your child about his/her dedication / baptism - what it meant to you and if there is any action they might like to take, eg. they might like to see their certificate or maybe get baptised or reaffirm their baptismal vows. Depending on the age of your child, get them involved in this process.

DAY TWENTY-FIVE: Praying together

READ: Ephesians 6:10-18

JOURNAL IDEA: Prayer is so powerful. You can put on your spiritual armour and be such a mighty warrior for your child. Write a warrior's prayer for your child.

PRAYER / ACTION: Find a way to pray with your child regularly. You could make a box of 'prayer tools': tokens and photos that prompt you to pray. It could include things like an acorn so you can pray to grow into 'oaks of righteousness' (Isaiah 61: 3); a little sword to use 'the sword of the spirit'; photos of people you love and other tokens as reminders of biblical truth; a little key maybe and ask God to give you some keys for the week; or a little crown and ask God to help you live like an heir etc. These tools make prayer more of an action and helps children, teenagers and even adults engage with it. It can also enable good and Godly discussions without having a 'forced' bible study.

DAY TWENTY-SIX:
Invest in good friendships

READ: Proverbs 22:24-25

JOURNAL IDEA: Write a list of families, children, communities that you would consider a good influence on your child. Consider / plan ways to spend time with them.

PRAYER / ACTION: If the church you are attending does not work well for your child, it might be worth prayerfully considering finding one that your child will love and where there is good age-appropriate provision. If this is not possible for you as a family, then invest in some holidays with others who have faith. Make it easy for your child to find good life-long friends with similar faith and values to you. Pray too that God will send some wonderful faith filled friends to walk alongside your child throughout their life.

DAY TWENTY-SEVEN: Encouragement

READ: Acts 20:2

JOURNAL IDEA: It is a well-researched fact that children flourish in an environment of encouragement. Think of ways that you could speak words of encouragement to your child or declare things over them that make them feel great about themselves. Sometimes it is hard to find the right words so you could write some down to store up for future use: 'you clever thing!'; 'you have such a great imagination'; 'how did you manage to get so tall?'; 'I love the way your mind works'; 'it's really impressive how much work you have put into...'; 'it makes my heart warm to see how kind you are to your friend'.

PRAYER / ACTION: Be proactive in cheering on your child. Give encouragement freely and also seek out other adults to join in. Grandparents, godparents, aunts and uncles have such a significant role to play in this area. You can even prompt them with some good questions to ask your children, such as 'show me how you did that'. It makes them feel important and heard, and that they have something to bring to the discussion.

DAY TWENTY-EIGHT:
Wisdom and favour

READ: Luke 2:52

JOURNAL IDEA: EVEN Jesus grew in wisdom and favour with the Lord! That is a prayer we can get behind! Take some time to write about what that might look like for your family.

PRAYER / ACTION: Wisdom is something you can simply ask the Lord for (James 1:5). Ask the Lord for the gift of wisdom for you and your child. It is amazing how some children really are very wise. You could also do some research into what favour is and how it works in God's wonderful kingdom.

DAY TWENTY-NINE: Forgiveness

READ: Matthew 6:12

JOURNAL IDEA: When we forgive others, we ourselves become free. Are there any people you need to forgive - maybe even your partner or your child or yourself? Take some time to start the process. Then think about how you might be able to model forgiveness to your child.

PRAYER / ACTION: If there are things you have held onto for a while, or people you have struggled to forgive, find a private space and imagine you are holding your unforgiveness in your clenched fist. Slowly open it and release forgiveness to them. Forgiveness is a process. Repeat this a few times until you feel free. Then teach this process to your child.

Note: If unforgiveness is something you are really struggling with, it is worth speaking to someone else about it. No matter how hard or how painful the situation is, until you can let go, you will always be the one who is bound.

DAY THIRTY: Treasures in heaven

READ: Matthew 6:19-21

JOURNAL IDEA: Write a list of the things that are most valuable to you and why. These can be material things but hopefully your list will include precious relationships and memories too. What would you like your child to treasure?

PRAYER / ACTION: Friends are a huge blessing and we are 'richer' for them. This is a wonderful way of understanding true treasure. Think about ways you could help your child store up treasure.

DAY THIRTY-ONE: God's superpowers

READ: Galatians 5:22-23

JOURNAL IDEA: We call the fruit of the Spirit 'God's superpowers'. Use your journal today to call out these 'powers' in yourself and your child.

PRAYER / ACTION: On the way to school or at the breakfast table, ask your child each day which superpower he/she would like. Then together pray that into them. It is a fun way to help them know what things God really values.

(And remember that joy has an extra secret power attached to it - strength! 'The joy of the Lord is my strength' (see Nehemiah 8:10).

DAY THIRTY-TWO: Lunch box love

READ: Proverbs 16:24

JOURNAL IDEA: How wonderful! Think of little things you can do and say to bring healing to little bones. As our children grow up and become increasingly independent, there are so many more places where they can get wounded by words - sometimes it is just a careless remark that can hurt the most. One of our jobs is to feed their souls and speak gracious words to heal their bones. Write about ways you could do this for your child.

PRAYER / ACTION: You could hide a little note in your child's lunchbox or put a post-it note hidden in their school bag or on their pillow. The notes could be a little joke or something that will make them laugh or a little encouragement like 'you are so kind!'. Think of little things that you can do that cost nothing that will fill up your child's love tank.

DAY THIRTY-THREE: Giving

READ: 2 Corinthians 9:7

JOURNAL IDEA: Use this time to reassess your finances, looking at what you give, how you give and how much of that your child sees / is involved with. Finance in the kingdom of God is so much more fun than we think.

Giving generously makes you feel good inside.

PRAYER / ACTION: Help your child to see the joy and blessing that comes with being generous: with money, with time and with our things. This simple lesson in giving could make them the richest people on earth!

DAY THIRTY-FOUR: Family values

READ: John 12:3

JOURNAL IDEA: Mary had all her priorities right. She knew that wherever she put her treasure that is where her heart would be (Matthew 6:21). Think about the 'values' which define your family, eg. hospitality, kindness, thankfulness, courage. Ask the Lord to help you define some values that are priorities in your household and how you can practise them together.

PRAYER / ACTION: Ask three questions of each other regularly that link to your values (perhaps at night before bed or at the supper table): what are you thankful for? When were you kind today? When were you brave? These values can become an integral part of your family life and identity. Find a practical way to engage with other values you may identify for your household, eg. if creativity is a high value, maybe once a week do something creative together.

DAY THIRTY-FIVE:
Kind words and anxiety

READ: Proverbs 12:25

JOURNAL IDEA: It is amazing how powerful kind words can be. Philippians 4 tells us not to be anxious about anything. But perhaps you are modelling anxiety to your child? It is so difficult to parent well when we are under high levels of stress. Sometimes simply being honest with your child is the best solution. Take this time to give any anxiety to the Lord afresh and consider how you can talk to your child about it without putting anxiety onto them. Then consider how your kind words can bring cheer to an anxious heart.

PRAYER / ACTION: Be proactive in speaking kind words to your child and others. You could go further and do some random acts of kindness with your child. Send someone a card, flowers or a gift; buy someone a coffee; help someone practically. There are so many ways you can show kindness. You could then discuss how great it makes your own heart feel!

SECTION FOUR

Trials and tribulations

Every family has areas of contention or difficulty. For many, a big area of stress is over screen time and, whilst compared with so many other issues in life it should be trivial, it can become destructive to relationships and results in much heartache. Learning to navigate these 'trivial' issues well as a family unit will stand you in good stead for when real hardships set in. This section addresses some specific areas and provides some practical ideas too.

Hundreds and hundreds of pages could be written just for this section, but the principles in each case are the same: invite Jesus right into the centre of the difficulty; try to look at each situation through God's eyes; take responsibility for your own actions; choose to trust God and don't let fear, anger, sadness or anxiety dictate how you behave.

Note: these suggestions are very simplistic solutions to some very hard situations. We parent as best we can and then we trust the Lord with ALL our hearts for our children and ourselves.

DAY THIRTY-SIX:
Mistakes and handling failure

READ: Romans 8:1-3

JOURNAL IDEA: How do you cope when your children make mistakes or let you down or fail in some way? These are normal parts of life but can raise so many issues. How do you get the balance right between discipline and comfort? How do you help your child discern the difference between conviction and condemnation? (Conviction is from God and leads to repentance and change. Condemnation is not from God and usually makes you feel like a terrible person, ie it becomes about who you are instead of about the bad action you may have performed. When you feel condemned you usually feel like there is no way back).

PRAYER / ACTION: The best way to deal with these sorts of issues is to plan ahead! Talk to your child about how they make choices, about failure and about discipline before it happens. It is good to have honest open discussions before shame and secrecy take a place in their hearts or minds. Mealtime discussions are good opportunities to throw in some hard questions around this subject.

Another great way to help your child understand failure or the consequences of mistakes is to read biographies with them. There are many wonderful stories of people who made mistakes but their lives were turned around.

DAY THIRTY-SEVEN: Screen time

READ: Philippians 4:8-9

JOURNAL IDEA: Decide with the Lord what is acceptable watching time and viewing material for you and your family. Take stock of where the screens are, who uses them and when.

PRAYER / ACTION: Chat through issues around screens, games and programmes with your partner and family. You could make a family contract about it, but be prepared to make some changes yourself! This is a major area of conflict in many families and you may need to discuss why those boundaries are necessary. You could include discussions around age-appropriate material, how screens can affect brain development and mental health, or issues around unrealistic comparison to 'perfect' lives and 'perfect' bodies. It may mean investing more than one discussion or prayer session around it.

Philippians 4 is a really great rule of thumb… if what you are watching (and reading) is not noble, right, pure, lovely, admirable etc then maybe it isn't something your eyes need to see? Remember, it is very difficult to 'unsee' things (which is one of the reasons why pornography is so destructive).

DAY THIRTY-EIGHT: Exasperation

READ: Ephesians 6:4

JOURNAL IDEA: We can often find ourselves feeling regularly exasperated, let alone our children! Write a prayer to the Lord asking him to show you the times you may have exasperated your child, then ask God to forgive you. God is good and kind and he will forgive you. Then ask him for the resources and patience to move forward.

PRAYER / ACTION: Commit to assessing your approach to discipline to ensure you are not exasperating your child. The Passion Translation of this verse talks about 'loving discipline' that 'brings the revelation of the Lord'. Pray about ways to bring revelation of the Lord to your child so that the Lord steps in before you have to!

DAY THIRTY-NINE: Bedtime / Bad Dreams / Peaceful Sleep

READ: Psalm 4:8

JOURNAL IDEA: This is often a very vulnerable place for both parents and children. Disrupted sleep can bring out the worst in all of us. Use your journal time to research all the places in the bible where God speaks about peaceful sleep. Then stand on the truth for you and your household. If necessary, actually stand on the page you have written as a prophetic act!

PRAYER / ACTION: If bedtime or sleep is tricky for your child (whatever age), start by building a really calm and stable bedtime routine with them. Write out this verse above their bed or put it under their pillow and pray God's incredible peace over them each evening.

It can really help to talk about or write down the things they are worrying about before they go to bed and to learn some deep breathing techniques to help relax. This works for adults and children alike.

Note: It may be necessary to do some of the earlier steps in reclaiming your house, such as inviting angels and playing worship music throughout the day to change the atmosphere. Look prayerfully at any pictures, posters or toys in the bedroom and remove any that you think may not be promoting peace.

DAY FORTY: Temper tantrums

READ: 1 Corinthians 13:5

JOURNAL IDEA: It can be hard to work out how to help our children manage their temper (often our own appears more often than we would like!). Ask God to reveal to you some of the triggers for your child's anger.

PRAYER / ACTION: Find a way to talk to your child about their anger when they are not angry (or hungry or tired!). Help them to recognise the stages in their anger and offer them tools to prevent an 'explosion', eg. when you feel the anger rising up, encourage them to ask 'please can I go to my room for 10 minutes?' Suggest other safe ways to vent their engergy. You can even give the stages of their anger names, eg. the image of a volcano: dormant, spewing lava, spewing gasses and exploding! Then you quickly learn what stage they are in and can diffuse the situation before getting to an explosion!

Most children do not like themselves when they are angry and can feel shame and great sadness afterwards – make room on your lap or in your heart to fill them up with love and forgiveness after the explosion.

Note: Do not despair, anger itself originates in the character of God and is a reaction to injustice, oppression and sin and leads to a passion for change and holiness.

DAY 41: Dealing with bereavement

READ: John 14:1-4

JOURNAL IDEA: When there is a bereavement in the family it is very hard to know how to help, especially if you are dealing with your own grief. Grief can also come through moving schools, friends moving away, loosing a loved toy or even not being chosen for a team. Take some time to ask the Lord how you should engage with the sadness in a healthy way for your child. Ask God to send you the Comforter - the Holy Spirit - to be with you.

PRAYER / ACTION: Grief is not something you can fix or control and it can often appear in unexpected ways. In as much as you can, put GRACE and LOVE at the top of the agenda. All other things will eventually come back into place but in the moment, chocolate for breakfast might be the only thing that gets you all through! It's OK to sit and cry with your child. Remember the good things about the person (or pet) and give thanks to God for them. Make a memory box. Be as available as you can be. Don't underestimate your child's sadness even if they move on quickly from moments of grief. Then repeat the process for as long as you need.

Note: If it is the loss of a parent or sibling or someone else close, it is advisable to seek some professional counsel for both you and your child.

DAY 42: Calling in the 'prodigals'

READ: Luke 15:20

JOURNAL IDEA: The parent of the prodigal only has one role - to keep their heart soft towards their child. This is such a powerful story. Write about what you can do to ensure your child understands that no matter what they have done you will always have space for them in your heart.

"The Prodigal mum!"

PRAYER / ACTION: Thank God for your 'prodigal' child. Forgive them. Speak God's truth over them and call them back in prayer! Wait for them with open arms.

DAY 43: Leaving home

READ: Psalm 121

JOURNAL IDEA: Whether your child is leaving home for good or simply on a new adventure for the day, it can be hard to let them go. This Psalm brings so much reassurance – write out the verses that YOU need to hold on to and release your child to God.

PRAYER / ACTION: Write this Psalm out and give it to your child to take with them with a note telling them how much you love them. If they are not the sort to appreciate bible verses (!) then write it and hide it in their luggage. There may be a quiet moment on their journey when they will be grateful to find it. They may never thank you but it may be that your action has made a huge difference to the course of their life or the decisions they make.

DAY 44: Difficult discussions

READ: John 8:32

JOURNAL IDEA: Think of some difficult discussions you have had in the past. What aspects of them were good and what were bad? Were you able to be honest and where necessary, agree to disagree? Telling the truth is always better in the long run.

PRAYER / ACTION: When there is a family argument, it helps to practise listening and give space to hear both sides to ensure you really understand each other before acting or responding. It is sometimes necessary to listen out for the underlying issue. If your child is disproportionately upset about something quite small, it may be that they are feeling insecure and empty but don't know how to articulate it.

Listening is a skill you can learn. Wherever possible, telling the whole truth to our child is usually the best way to address difficult issues. Our children then learn that the door is always open for awkward discussions in the future.

DAY 45: Buckets of grace

READ: 2 Corinthians 13:11-14

JOURNAL IDEA: We need buckets of grace to be great mothers. What would it look like for your family to have the GRACE of the Lord Jesus Christ?

PRAYER / ACTION: Why not occasionally surprise your child and let them do something 'wild', eg. pudding before main course; watch TV for longer than usual; stay up late; buy something special; go to the sweet shop; wear fancy dress to church - or anything that would bring them great joy!

OTHER PRACTICAL IDEAS TO MAKE YOU A SUPERMUM!

SIDE BY SIDE

Talking while walking side by side or sitting in a car often takes the pressure off conversations. Face to face conversations can get quite intense. Use car journeys or walks to have conversations or pray with your child regularly. They may feel more able to speak about difficult things when you don't appear to be intensely focused on them.

SPEAKING BLESSINGS AND TRUTH

Learn to speak blessings, declarations and truth over your child. Do it when you are with them, when you are not with them and over them when they are asleep. Don't worry if your child is not living at home anymore – God is not limited by distance or time. Use scripture when you can, eg. Numbers 6:24-26 or Ephesians 3:14-21, and speak it directly over them as a prayer or use it to call out truth in your child: 'I know that God made you like Joshua in the bible, to be strong and courageous, you don't need to be anxious' etc.

CREATE MEMORIES

Be proactive in creating great memories for your child. These do not need to cost anything, eg. home movie nights, outdoor adventures, a kitchen disco, pretending to have a power cut, games nights, family sleepover (all sleep in one room), lighting fires, camping etc.

LAUGH AND LAUGH AND LAUGH

Find things that make your child laugh and then laugh with them, eg. good movies, watching you dance (!), reading joke books - anything good. Laughter is so healing.

FILL THEIR LOVE TANKS

Work out what makes them feel loved and then pour your love into them even if it is costly to you: with words, with actions, with time, with healthy physical touch. Find whatever it takes to love them completely.

PUT DOWN YOUR PHONE

Put down your phone and focus on them!

CREATE HEALTHY ROUTINES AND BOUNDARIES

While this may be hard, this is a great way to give your child stability. It is like the rules in a sports game - it gives your child freedom to play well.

READ WITH YOUR CHILDREN

No matter what age or stage your children are, there is something really special about reading out loud together or simply being together in the same space, each with a book. You could read stories that engage them or try them on biographies of great people. Audio books are also an easy way to enjoy a book together. Books open minds, help discover new worlds or countries; books inform conversations and stretch the boundaries of possibility. Reading gives your child confidence to stand tall in almost any situation.

IDEAS FOR FAMILY PRAYER AND BIBLE READING

For younger children not keen on praying, find a toy they love and give it a voice. Then ask the toy if he wants to pray. Be the voice of the toy and pray something very simple like 'God help me to be kind today'. Then begin to get the toy praying regularly in his own voice. At some point you can ask your child if the toy wants to pray and he/she might make the toy pray. Bingo! You have your child praying, even if it's through the voice of a toy!

Make reading the bible fun and as regular as you can by modelling it. Find a version of the bible that is appropriate for their age and stage. Then as much as you can bring it to life. Read the stories, act them out or draw pictures about them. Find images or verses that convey a biblical message or theme and have them accessible in the house or on your walls.

Pick a verse or a chapter or a theme and make it the 'Verse of the week / month' and chat about it, memorise it, make it relevant to them. Helping your child memorise scripture is such a great investment for their future and yours!

Whatever you do, try to make the bible a central part of everyday living.

SCHOOL / COLLEGE / UNIVERSITY

While your children are still in education (but it could also be appropriate for their work place) take an interest in the people they talk about and pray for them by name. If there isn't already a parent's prayer group, why not start one?

A FINAL WORD

Father God loves you unconditionally, he knows you completely and he chose you. You are wonderfully made in his image. Put aside your fears, anxiety, comparisons, control and anything else that might be getting in the way. You have what it takes to be the mum that your child needs. None of us are perfect and none of us get it right all of the time. Forgive yourself quickly, straighten your crown and keep going!

Remember **YOU ARE NOT ALONE!** God is walking beside you and will give you all that you need. Reach out for his hand on the tough days and find some other mums to do this journey with too!

A big thank you to Mike and Joshua, Jo, Sarah, Emma, Michelle, Philly and Tab and all the other 'Wonder Women' in my life. Thank you for cheering me on and helping me be the best 'me' I can be!

PS. If you enjoyed this journal please do look at my website: www.perry-may.com to see my growing number or resources to build and enhance connection with the Lord for individuals, families and groups.

Printed in Great Britain
by Amazon

61784427R00063